Northern New England

MAINE • NEW HAMPSHIRE • VERMONT

By
Thomas G. Aylesworth
Virginia L. Aylesworth

CHELSEA HOUSE PUBLISHERS
New York   Philadelphia

Created and produced by Blackbirch Graphics, Inc.

PROJECT EDITOR: Bruce S. Glassman
ASSOCIATE EDITOR: Robin Langley Sommer
DESIGN: Richard S. Glassman

3   5   7   9   8   6   4   2

Printed in the United States

Library of Congress Cataloging-in-Publication Data

Aylesworth, Thomas G.
  Northern New England.

  (Let's discover the states)
  Includes bibliographies and index.
  Summary: Discusses the geographical, historical, and cultural aspects of Maine, Vermont, and New
Hampshire, using maps, illustrated fact spreads, and other illustrated material to highlight the land, history,
and people of each individual state.
    1. New England—Juvenile literature.   2. Maine—Juvenile literature.   3. Vermont—Juvenile
literature.   4. New Hampshire—Juvenile literature.   [1. New England.   2. Maine.   3. Vermont.   4. New
Hampshire]   I. Aylesworth, Virginia L.   II. Title.   III. Series.
Aylesworth, Thomas G. Let's discover the states.
F4.3.A95   1988   974   87-17869
ISBN 1-55546-551-X
      0-7910-0538-0 (pbk.)

CONTENTS

VERMONT

Tall spires on white clapboard churches reaching for
   the sky.
Waves pounding the rock-bound coast of the Atlantic
   Ocean.
Lobstermen mending their traps on a pier.
The gingerbread facade of the Wedding Cake House in
   Kennebunk.
Skiers whizzing down the slopes of Sugarloaf
   Mountain near Kingfield.
Hundreds of logs clogging the Kennebec River on their
   way to the mills.

Let's Discover
Maine

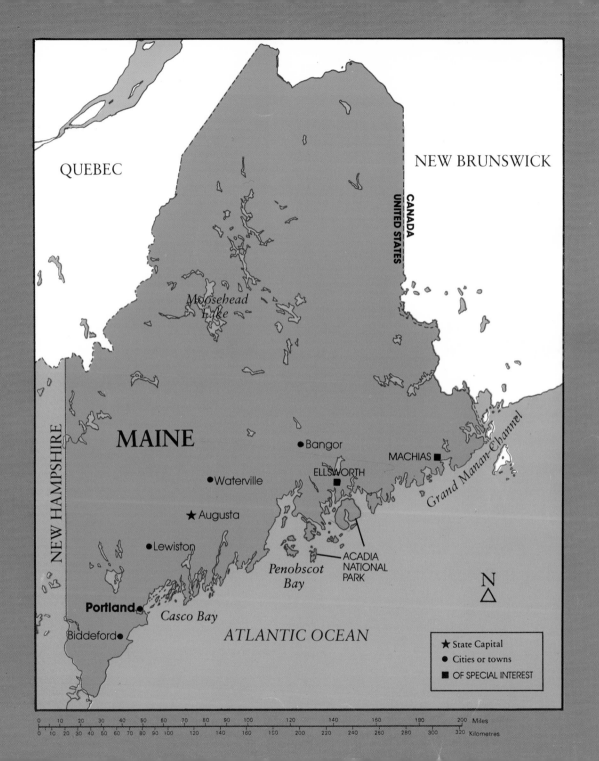

MAINE
At a Glance

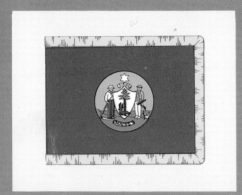

State Flag

Capital: Augusta

Major Industries: Paper and wood products, textiles, fishing

Major Crops: Potatoes, apples, sweet corn, blueberries

State Bird: Chickadee

State Flower: White Pine Cone and Tassel

Size: 33,215 square miles (39th largest)

Population: 1,156,000 (38th largest)

The White Mountains region of Maine covers the northern section of the state. It is in this area that the rugged landscape becomes more heavily forested and dotted with lakes.

The Land

Maine is bordered on the west by New Hampshire and the Canadian province of Quebec, on the north by the Canadian provinces of Quebec and New Brunswick, on the east by New Brunswick, and on the south by the Atlantic Ocean. The state has three main land regions: the Coastal Lowlands, the Eastern New England Upland, and the White Mountains Region.

The Coastal Lowlands form a strip along Maine's Atlantic shoreline. They are part of a larger land area that stretches along the entire New England coast. In the south there are broad, sandy beaches that give way to salt marshes. In the north are small bays along a rocky coast dominated by high cliffs. Sand, gravel, granite, and limestone are important mineral resources here. Fishermen and lobstermen sail from ports along the Coastal Lowlands, and farmers raise blueberries, beef cattle, and poultry in the region. Off the coast are thousands of islands, of which the largest is Mount Desert.

The Eastern New England Upland is northwest of the Coastal Lowlands. It is part of a shelflike formation that extends from Canada to Connecticut. In Maine, the area rises to several thousand feet above sea level. The Aroostook Plateau, in the northeast, has rich soil in which the famous Maine potatoes are grown. Dairy and beef cattle thrive here, and forestry is another important industry of the region.

Maine has more than 3,000 miles of coastline. Sea-related industries are very important to the state and fishermen and lobstermen have depended on the ocean for their livelihood for centuries.

The mountainous areas of Maine are a popular attraction for skiing enthusiasts every year.

Casco Bay, near Portland, is one of the many large bays, coves, and inlets that comprise the state's coastline.

The White Mountains Region covers northwestern Maine and extends into New Hampshire and Vermont. This mountainous area has hundreds of lakes and a series of eskers, or low gravel ridges formed during the Ice Age. Forest products and maple syrup are the main sources of livelihood in the region.

Maine's coastline is 228 miles long, but if the bays, coves, inlets and island shorelines are included, it measures 3,478 miles. The state has more than 5,000 rivers and streams. The chief rivers are the Androscoggin, Saco, Kennebec, Penobscot, and St. John. There are more than 2,500 lakes and ponds in Maine, which is the largest New England state. Its highest point is 5,268-foot Mount Katahdin, in central Maine.

Maine's annual precipitation is between 35 and 45 inches, much of it falling as snow during the winter months. Summers are short and relatively cool; winters are cold and long. The coastal areas are relatively temperate, with Portland having an average January temperature of 21 degrees Fahrenheit and an average July temperature of 68 degrees F. Weather changes are often sudden and severe. The northern forests may have winter temperatures below 0 degrees F. and up to 100 inches of snow per year.

The History

Before the arrival of European explorers, thousands of Indians lived in what would become the state of Maine. Most of them belonged to the Algonquian language family. They included the Penobscots, the Passamaquoddies, and the Abnaki tribe, which lived west of the Penobscot River. The Etchemin lived east of the river. Sometimes their villages were raided by Iroquois people from what is now New York state.

There is evidence that the first Europeans to arrive in the Maine area were members of a Viking expedition led by Leif Ericson, who may have landed about A.D. 1000. The next visitor of record was John Cabot, an Italian sea captain in the service of the English, who probably arrived in 1498. Cabot was followed in 1524 by the Italian Giovanni da Verrazano, employed by the French. The Frenchmen Pierre du Guast and Samuel de Champlain both arrived in 1604. Maine's first non-Indian settlement was founded by the French on St. Croix Island in 1604 but it lasted for only one winter.

An Englishman, George Waymouth, explored the Maine coast in 1605 on behalf of two wealthy countrymen, Sir Ferdinando Gorges and Sir John Popham. They were so impressed with Waymouth's description of the area that they sent a group of colonists to the New World in 1607. This group established Popham Plantation near the mouth of the Kennebec River. The settlement lasted only about a year, during which time the colonists built America's first transatlantic trading ship, the *Virginia*. In 1608 cold weather and other hardships forced the settlers to return to England. The British established another colony near present-day Saco in 1623, and others followed later in the decade.

In 1622 Gorges and another Englishman, John Mason, were given a large tract of land by the Council for New England, which was an

Navigator Sebastian Cabot
and his father, John Cabot,
made landings on the Maine
coast in the late 1490s. Italian
by birth, they were employed
by England to find a sea route
to the Indies, and their voyage
of 1497 gave England a strong
claim to the North American
mainland, including what is
now Canada. After his father's
death, Sebastian Cabot sailed
west again in search of a
passage across the northern
edge of the New World. His
explorations resulted in some
of the most accurate maps of
the 16th century.

agency of the British government. The grant included a large part of what is now Maine and New Hampshire. In 1629 the two men divided the territory, and Gorges took the Maine section. He established a government in 1636, and in 1641 he made the town of Gorgeana (now York) a city—the first chartered English city in what is now the United States.

Gorges died in 1647, and the towns of Kittery, Wells, and York united under a new government. By 1658 these three towns, along with Casco Bay, Kennebunk, Saco, and Scarborough, had joined the Massachusetts Bay Colony. The heirs of Ferdinando Gorges objected that the Maine area was theirs, and in 1664 an English board of commissioners returned Maine to the Gorges family. The dispute was resolved when Massachusetts bought the area from them for about $6,000 in 1677.

Between 1689 and 1763, the French and Indian Wars brought conflict to Maine and all of New England, as the British vied with the French and their Indian allies for the territory. When the wars ended, France gave up its claims to Maine and most of North America to the British.

During the 1760s, the people of Maine and the other colonies objected to taxes and trade restrictions imposed by the British government to pay for the colonial wars. There was even a "York Tea Party" in 1774, when a group of Maine men burned a supply of British tea in that town. When the Revolutionary War began in 1775, hundreds of men from Maine joined the Continental Army. The British retaliated by blocking trade in Maine, which caused a shortage of food and other necessities. The British also burned the town of Falmouth (present-day Portland) in 1775, as punishment for opposition to colonial policy.

The first naval battle of the Revolutionary War was fought off Machias in 1775, when Maine men captured the British ship *Margaretta*. That same year, General Benedict Arnold and his men set out from Augusta to attack Quebec, but they were repulsed by the British. In 1779 British troops took the town of Castine.

French explorer, fur trader, cartographer, and colonizer Samuel de Champlain explored much of the Maine coast early in the 17th century. Champlain founded the city of Quebec in 1608 and laid the foundations for what was called New France (now Canada).

After the war ended in 1783, Massachusetts gave parts of the Maine area to war veterans in place of back pay, and population increased. The pine forests were Maine's economic backbone in the early 1800s: they were used to create a thriving shipbuilding industry. Trade with other countries flourished until 1807, when the Embargo Act slowed down the shipping industry but fostered the growth of manufacturing to offset the economic loss.

After the War of 1812, the movement to separate Maine from Massachusetts found many supporters. Maine residents voted for separation in 1819, and in 1820 Maine entered the Union as the 23rd state, with Portland as its capital. Augusta became the capital in 1832. Maine's admission was affected by the Missouri Compromise, by which Missouri was admitted as a slave state and Maine as a free state in order to maintain the balance between slave and free states. In 1842 a long-standing dispute about the Maine boundary with Canada was resolved by the Webster-Ashburton Treaty.

Anti-slavery feelings were strong in Maine for 30 years before the Civil War broke out in 1861. Some 72,000 Maine men joined the Union Army during the conflict, and the nation's vice-president during Abraham Lincoln's first term was Hannibal Hamlin, who had served as Maine's governor.

After the war, Maine industry prospered, especially textiles and leather goods. During the 1890s, the state's many rivers were utilized for generating hydroelectric power. Throughout the early 1900s, the number of small farms in the state decreased, and many large farms were started; they specialized in the cultivation of potatoes and in dairy and poultry products. Paper and pulp industries began to take up the industrial slack created by the relocation of many textile factories to the South, where labor was cheaper.

During the 1940s, one of the best-known political figures in Washington was a Maine woman, Margaret Chase Smith. She was the first woman to win election to the House of Representatives and then to the Senate.

During World War II, about 95,000 men and women from Maine served in the armed forces. Boots, shoes and military uniforms poured from Maine's factories. Cargo and combat ships were built at Bath and South Portland. During the 1950s Air Force bases were constructed in the state, increasing the population of surrounding communities.

Today, Maine continues its economic growth. Industry and agriculture are well balanced, and the state has become a favorite with tourists, who spent $700 million per year in the mid-1980s. Maine is known for having the highest tides, the tastiest potatoes, and the tartest conversations in the country ("Down Easters," as Maine residents are called, are famous for not wasting words). Their nickname probably originated from the early New England use of the word "down" to mean "north."

The first school in Maine may have been at an Indian mission founded in 1696. The first school for settlers opened in York in 1701, but tax-supported schools did not begin until 1868. By the time Maine became a state, it had two institutions of higher education: Bowdoin College (1794) and Colby College (1813). The University of Maine was established in 1865.

Much of Portland's economic growth came during World War II when its factories produced uniforms for the war effort. The city is still one of Maine's centers of industry.

Revolutionary War general Henry Knox made his home in Thomaston, in a grand mansion he called Montpelier. As a colonel in the Continental Army, fought under George Washington at the Battle of Trenton (1776) and was promoted to brigadier general. In 1785 he became the nation's first secretary of war.

The People

Slightly more than 47 percent of the people of Maine live in towns or cities such as Portland, Lewiston, and Bangor. Most of them were born in the United States. The largest single religious denomination is the Roman Catholic, but there are more Protestants than Catholics in Maine, most of them Baptists, Episcopalians, Methodists, and members of the United Church of Christ.

Poet Henry Wadsworth Longfellow was born in Portland. He is perhaps best remembered for his verse on Indian life entitled "The Song of Hiawatha". One of his finest poems, "The Cross of Snow," was written as a tribute to his wife 18 years after her accidental death. Longfellow was the first American to be honored in the Poet's Corner of London's Westminster Abbey.

Several important political figures have come from Maine. One of them was legislator Margaret Chase Smith, born in Skowhegan. Another was Hannibal Hamlin (Paris Hill), who was one of America's leading abolitionists before the Civil War and served as vice-president under Lincoln.

In the field of letters, Maine has contributed two of our greatest poets. Henry Wadsworth Longfellow, author of "The Song of Hiawatha" and "The Village Blacksmith," was born in Portland. Edna St. Vincent Millay, who won a Pulitzer Prize for "The Harp-Weaver," was a native of Rockland.

Dorothea Dix, the celebrated social reformer who fought for humane treatment of the mentally ill and of prisoners, was a native of Hampden. Hiram Stevens Maxim, inventor of the first automatic gun, was born in Brockway's Mills, and his brother Hudson Maxim, who also developed new kinds of munitions, was born in Orneville.

Hampden native Dorothea
Dix began a nationwide
campaign to improve
conditions for prisoners, the
mentally retarded, and the
mentally ill in 1841.
Advocating a humane
approach to the treatment of
mental illness, she was
instrumental in establishing
more than 30 health care
facilities.

The Henry Wadsworth
Longfellow House.

OF SPECIAL INTEREST

ON THE SOUTHEAST COAST: *Acadia National Park*
This beautiful seashore area includes Mount Desert Island and several smaller
    islands along with part of the Schoodic Peninsula.

IN ELLSWORTH: *Black Mansion*
Built about 1820, this stately home resembles George Washington's Virginia estate,
    Mount Vernon.

IN MACHIAS: *Burnham Tavern*
It was here that the Maine men met in 1775 to plot the capture of the British ship
    Margaretta.

NEAR PORTLAND: *Portland Head Light*
This towering 101-foot lighthouse, built to guide mariners in 1791, affords a
    magnificent view of the surf-beaten rocks.

IN PORTLAND: *Wadsworth Longfellow House*
This three-story brick building was the boyhood home of one of America's best-
    loved poets, Henry Wadsworth Longfellow.

For more information write:
CHAMBER OF COMMERCE AND INDUSTRY
126 SEWALL STREET
AUGUSTA, MAINE 04330

FURTHER READING

Bailey, Bernadine. *Picture Book of Maine*, rev. ed. Whitman, 1967.
Berchen, William. *Maine*. Houghton Mifflin, 1973.
Carpenter, Allan. *Maine*, rev. ed. Childrens Press, 1979.
Clark, Charles E. *Maine: A Bicentennial History*. W.W. Norton, 1977.
Fradin, Dennis B. *Maine in Words and Pictures*. Childrens Press, 1980.
Isaacson, Doris A., ed. *Maine: A Guide "Down East,"* 2nd ed. Maine State
    Museum, 1970.

The rainbow colors of fall foliage on a mountainside.
Democracy in action at a traditional New England
town meeting.
Giant ice sculptures at the Winter Carnival on the
Dartmouth College campus.
Towering trees and cliffs above the deep chasm at
Franconia Notch.
The sound of surf and the tang of salt air on White
Sand Beach at Rye.
Dairy cows grazing on the green pastures around Lake
Winnipesaukee.

Let's Discover

New

Hampshire

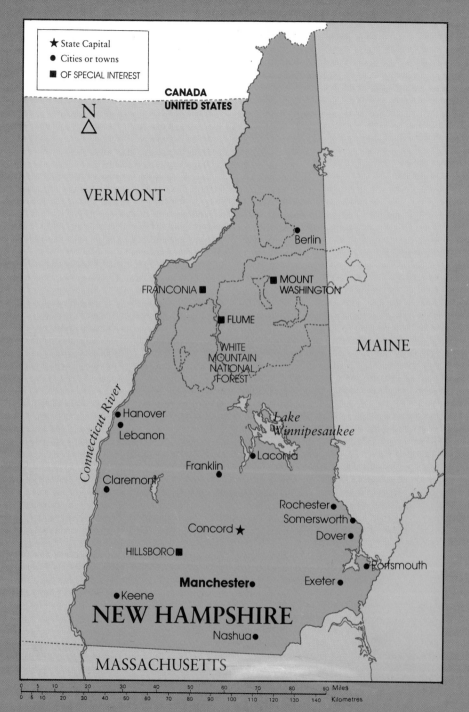

★ State Capital
● Cities or towns
■ OF SPECIAL INTEREST

CANADA
UNITED STATES

N

VERMONT

● Berlin

FRANCONIA ■

■ MOUNT WASHINGTON

■ FLUME

WHITE MOUNTAIN NATIONAL FOREST

MAINE

Connecticut River

● Hanover

● Lebanon

Lake Winnipesaukee

● Franklin

● Laconia

● Claremont

● Rochester
● Somersworth
● Dover

Concord ★

HILLSBORO ■

● Portsmouth

Manchester●

Exeter ●

● Keene

NEW HAMPSHIRE

Nashua ●

MASSACHUSETTS

0 5 10   20   30   40   50   60   70   80   90 Miles
0 5 10   20   30   40   50   60   70   80   90   100   110   120   130   140 Kilometres

State Bird: Purple Finch

State Flower: Purple Lilac

NEW HAMPSHIRE
At a Glance

Capital: Concord

State Flag

Size: 9,304 square miles (44th largest)

Population: 977,000 (41st largest)

Major Industries: Machinery, computers, forest products, tourism

Major Crops: Dairy products, hay, vegetables, apples, maple syrup

27

Squam Lake is in central New Hampshire. New Hampshire contains some 1,300 lakes and ponds, most of them created by the glacial activity of the Ice Age.

The Land

New Hampshire is bounded on the west by Vermont and the Canadian province of Quebec, on the north by Quebec, on the east by Maine and the Atlantic Ocean, and on the south by Massachusetts. The state has three main land regions: the Coastal Lowlands, the Eastern New England Upland, and the White Mountains Region.

Autumn brings magnificently colored foliage to the New Hampshire landscape. Forests cover some 80 percent of the state, and the changing color of their leaves attracts many visitors to see the bright yellows, reds, and oranges cover the hills and valleys.

The rugged terrain of the White Mountains provide exciting campsites for those who enjoy the outdoors.

New Hampshire has the harsh winters typical of northern New England. In the Mount Washington area, a season's snowfall of more than 12 feet is not uncommon.

The Coastal Lowlands are in southeastern New Hampshire, along the Atlantic Ocean. They are part of a larger region that follows the coast of the New England states and extends 15 to 20 miles inland. This is an area of fine beaches and abundant marine life, where fishermen operate their fleets. It also has poultry farms, orchards, and nurseries that grow ornamental plants for market.

The Eastern New England Upland covers the rest of southern New Hampshire from east to west and is part of the same hilly region that extends from northern Maine to eastern Connecticut. The Merrimack Valley, the Hills and Lakes Area, and the New Hampshire part of the Connecticut River Valley are in this region. Mills and factories operate here, as well as hay and fruit farms. Granite, sand, gravel, and mica are quarried in the region. Dairy cows and other livestock contribute to New Hampshire's economy.

The White Mountains Region occupies northern New Hampshire. These rugged mountains surround wide, flat areas that support vast forests of spruce, fir, and yellow birch. Lumbering and paper manufacturing are important industries, and dairy and potato farms thrive.

New Hampshire's major rivers are the Connecticut, the Pemigewasset, the Merrimack, the Androscoggin, the Saco, and the Piscataqua. There are about 1,300 lakes in the state, of which the largest is 72-square-mile Lake Winnipesaukee.

The climate of New Hampshire provides relatively short, cool summers and long, severe winters, with up to 150 inches of snow in the mountains. Several slopes in northern New Hampshire provide good spring skiing into April. Annual rainfall ranges from 50 inches in the mountains to about 35 inches near the coast. Concord, the capital, in the southeast, has an average January temperature of 22 degrees Fahrenheit and a July average of 70 degrees F. But in Berlin, in the northern mountains, the average January temperature is 14 degrees F. and the average July temperature is 66 degrees F.

The History

Before the arrival of European explorers, there were probably about 5,000 Indians living in what would become New Hampshire, primarily Abnaki and Pennacook groups whose members spoke Algonquian languages. The Abnaki group included the Ossipee and the Pequawket tribes. In the Pennacook group were the Amoskeag, Nashua, Piscataqua, Souhegan, and Squamscot tribes. All of them were hunters, fishermen, and farmers. They lived in wigwams made of bark and skins, and moved to new locations when fish and game grew scarce.

An Englishman named Martin Pring is the first European known to have explored any part of New Hampshire. He reached the coast in 1603 and sailed up the Piscataqua River, perhaps landing at what is now Portsmouth. In 1605 came the Frenchman Samuel de Champlain, followed by the English captain John Smith, who landed in 1614 on the Isles of Shoals, which he named Smith's Islands.

King James I of England founded a Council for New England in 1620 to encourage settlement in the New World. David Thompson and a small group of colonists were granted lands in present-day New Hampshire, and they arrived near what is now Portsmouth in 1623. They founded a settlement called Odiorne's Point, which is now a part of Rye. At about the same time, another group led by Edward Hilton settled Hilton's Point (now Dover). George Mason named his large land grant between the Merrimack and Piscataqua rivers New Hampshire, for his Hampshire County birthplace in England. Towns sprang up in the area, chiefly along rivers, whose falls provided power for grain mills and sawmills that cut up the fine timber.

New Hampshire was made part of Massachusetts in 1641, but in 1680 Charles II made it a separate colony. During the French and Indian Wars, between 1689 and 1763, the British fought the French

THE PORTRAICTUER OF CAPTAYNE JOHN SMITH ADMIRALL OF NEW ENGLAND

The English explorer Captain John Smith spent several years traveling uncharted areas of New England after he helped found the colony of Jamestown, Virginia, in 1607. In 1614 he landed on New Hampshire's Isles of Shoals and renamed them Smith's Islands. His book *A Description of New England* guided the Pilgrims to Massachusetts.

and their Indian allies, and several New Hampshire colonists won renown as military leaders. Robert Rogers and John Stark helped defeat French invasions from Canada.

The citizens of New Hampshire, like the other colonists, became resentful of the restrictive trade policies and taxes imposed by England during the 1760s. Indeed, the Provincial Congress adopted a constitution making New Hampshire an independent colony in January 1776, six months before the Declaration of Independence was adopted. One of the first armed actions against the British occurred in New Hamshire in 1774, when John Sullivan led a band of colonists in seizing British military supplies from a fort in New Castle.

When the Revolutionary War broke out in Massachusetts in 1775, hundreds of New Hampshire militiamen rushed to Boston to take part in the fighting. Although New Hampshire was the only one of the 13 original colonies not invaded by the British, its men fought for eight

American naval officer and Revolutionary War hero John Paul Jones was one of New Hampshire's best-known residents during the 18th century. Jones, who lived in Portsmouth, is remembered for his determined response to a British demand to surrender during a naval engagement: "I have not yet begun to fight."

years on land and sea to bring about the victory. In 1788 New Hampshire became the ninth state to ratify the new Constitution of the United States.

After the Revolution, industry and trade became more important in New Hampshire. Ocean commerce on swift clipper ships and commercial fishing flourished. The first railroad was built in 1838. The 1850s brought hosiery plants, woolen mills, and factories that turned out boots, shoes, machine tools, and wood products.

Until the mid-1800s, almost everyone in New Hampshire was of British-colonial stock. Except for those towns with Indian names, most communities had names borrowed from England: Plymouth, Bristol, Concord, Manchester, Colebrook, Bath, Albany, and many more. But when the industrial boom began, a flood of French Canadians arrived to work in the factories.

New Hampshire was a hotbed of abolitionism before the Civil War. Anti-slavery sentiment was one of the factors that sent some 34,000 men from the state into service with Union forces. The Portsmouth Naval Yard turned out many blockade ships for the U.S. Navy between 1861 and 1865. After the war, the state's industrial growth continued, although agriculture remained important.

A view of Concord in 1852. In the mid-19th century, New Hampshire embarked upon a new era of industrial expansion.

35

Dartmouth College, New Hampshire's first college, was established in Hanover in 1769. In 1816 the college became the focus of a famous legal battle called the Dartmouth College Case. The conflict centered around the state's desire to take control of the college and to rename it Dartmouth University. Alumnus Daniel Webster argued the case for Dartmouth and won. The ruling, important in legal history, helped to establish the inviolability of contracts.

During World War I, which the United States entered in 1917, the Portsmouth Naval Yard produced many warships, and some 20,000 New Hampshire men served in the armed forces during the conflict. In the following decade, the cotton and woolen industries declined, due to cheaper labor in Southern mills, and leather and shoe manufacturing became the state's leading industries. New roads and hydroelectric plants were built.

Some 60,000 New Hampshire men and women served in the armed forces during World War II, and Portsmouth retained its status as a major New England port and shipbuilder during the years 1941 to 1945. The mills made thousands of military uniforms under government contracts to wartime industries.

Today, many segments of New Hampshire's economy are still growing. Electronics and precision instruments are among the newer industries, and tourism accounts for more than $4 billion in annual revenue. The state's beautiful beaches, mountains, and ski resorts attract visitors from all over the Northeast.

Some of the one-room schoolhouses established by early settlers still stand in New Hampshire. The first public-education laws were passed in 1789, and the state's first free library opened at Peterborough in 1833. New Hampshire's first institution of higher education was Dartmouth College, founded in 1769. The University of New Hampshire, established in 1866, was the second.

The People

More than 52 percent of the people in New Hampshire live in towns and cities such as Manchester, Nashua, and Concord. Most of them were born in the United States. The largest single religious body is the Roman Catholic Church. There are, however, more Protestants than Catholics in New Hampshire, including Baptists, Episcopalians, Methodists, Unitarian Universalists, and members of the United Church of Christ.

Franklin Pierce, the 14th president of the United States, was born in Hillsboro in 1804. During Pierce's tenure in the White House, the United States signed a trade treaty with Japan, purchased land on the Mexican border, and passed the Kansas-Nebraska Act, by which settlers in these two territories would decide for themselves whether to permit slavery.

Daniel Webster, born in Salisbury in 1782, was a renowned politician, diplomat, and lawyer of the early 19th century. One of the nation's ablest statesmen, he delivered stirring addresses that emphasized the power of the federal government over that of the individual states.

Journalist and social reform advocate Horace Greeley was born in Amherst in 1811. As publisher of the *New York Tribune*, Greeley advocated land reform and protective tariffs and opposed slavery. He popularized the slogan "Go west, young man."

Three important statesmen have come from New Hamsphire to take their places in American history. Franklin Pierce, the 14th president of the United States, was born in Hillsboro. The legendary orator and senator Daniel Webster was from Salisbury (now Franklin). Nineteenth-century jurist and abolitionist Salmon P. Chase was born in Cornish Township.

The founder of Christian Science, Mary Baker Eddy, was a native of Bow. The 19th-century journalist and politican Horace Greeley, who popularized the slogan "Go west, young man," was from Amherst. Astronaut Alan B. Shepard of East Derry became the first American to travel in space in 1961.

Far left:
Shakers, also called The United Society of Believers in Christ's Second Appearing, have been present in New Hampshire for about 200 years. The religious group derives its name from the "shaking and quaking" that accompanies revelations and spiritual experiences. Shaker Village, in Canterbury, offers visitors an opportunity to explore a traditional Shaker community.

At left:
Traditional craftsmanship is still valued in New Hampshire. The state's many arts-and-crafts fairs are popular events.

Daniel Webster's Birthplace.

OF SPECIAL INTEREST

NEAR FRANKLIN: *Daniel Webster's Birthplace*
This two-room cabin in scenic surroundings contains mementos of America's
best-known orator, who was born in 1782.

NEAR FRANCONIA: *The Old Man of the Mountain*
This craggy likeness of a man's profile was the inspiration for Nathaniel
Hawthorne's story "The Great Stone Face."

AT FRANCONIA NOTCH: *The Flume*
An 800-foot-long chasm through the scenic wilderness of the White Mountains.

IN HILLSBORO: *Franklin Pierce Homestead*
This large two-story house, built in 1804, has been preserved as it was when
President Pierce spent his early years here.

NEAR FABYAN HOUSE: *Mount Washington*
A 22-mile-long cog railway and a network of trails provide excellent views of the
highest peak in the Northeast.

For more information write:
NEW HAMPSHIRE VACATION CENTER
BOX 856
CONCORD, NEW HAMPSHIRE 03301

FURTHER READING

Bailey, Bernadine. *Picture Book of New Hampshire*, rev. ed. Whitman, 1971.
Carpenter, Allan. *New Hampshire*, rev. ed. Childrens Press, 1979.
Fradin, Dennis B. *New Hampshire in Words and Pictures*. Childrens Press, 1981.
Hill, Evan. *The Primary State: An Historical Guide to New Hamsphire*.
Countryman, 1976.
Lane, Paula, ed. *The New Hampshire Atlas and Gazetteer*, 2nd ed. DeLorme,
1979.
Morison, E. E. and Elizabeth F. *New Hampshire: A Bicentennial History*. W.W.
Norton, 1976.

The early-spring excitement of maple-sugar season.
Hills covered with the kaleidoscopic colors of fall
  foliage.
Sunlight gleaming from the golden dome of the state
  capitol in Montpelier.
The soaring tower of the Bennington Battle Monument.
The cool blue waters of Lake Champlain inviting
  vacationers to water sports.
Snow-capped winter peaks in the historic Green
  Mountains.

Let's Discover
Vermont

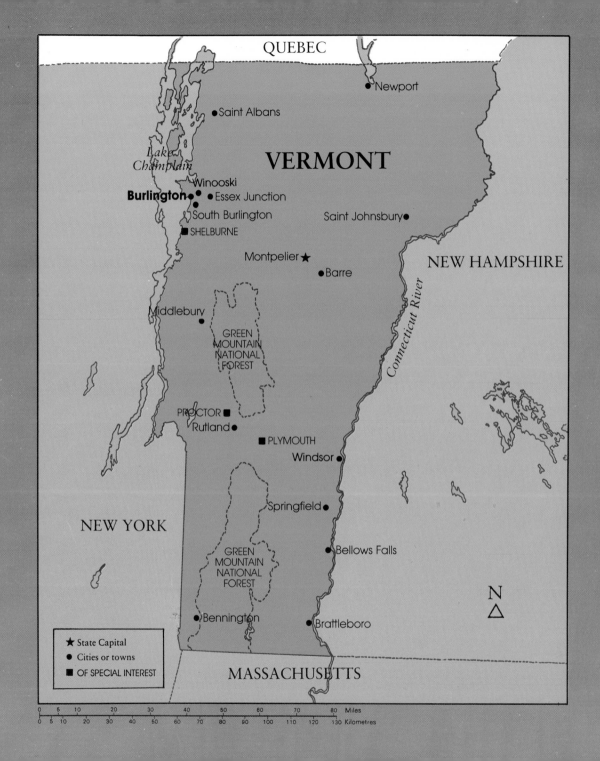

VERMONT
At a Glance

State Flag

Capital: Montpelier

Major Industries: Machine tools, furniture, stone quarrying, agriculture

Major Crops: Apples, maple syrup, hay

State Bird: Hermit Thrush

State Flower: Red Clover

Size: 9,609 square miles (43rd largest)

Population: 530,000 (48th largest)

45

North Ferrisburg, in northwestern Vermont, is part of the Champlain Valley. This area, on the banks of Lake Champlain, has some of the state's best farmland.

The Land

Vermont is bounded on the west by New York, on the north by the Canadian province of Quebec, on the east by New Hampshire, and on the south by Massachusetts. The state has six main land regions: the White Mountains, the Western New England Upland, the Green Mountains, the Vermont Valley, the Taconic Mountains, and the Champlain Valley.

The White Mountain Region is in the northeastern part of the state; Vermont shares these mountains with New Hampshire and Maine. The White Mountains include peaks that rise more than 3,000 feet, with many swift-running streams flowing between them. Potatoes are grown here, but the region is too hilly for extensive farming.

Northeastern Vermont contains high peaks and rocky lands nourished by swift rivers and streams. Some vegetables are grown here, but the region is too rugged for extensive farming.

The Western New England Upland comprises most of Vermont's eastern border area and extends into Massachusetts and Connecticut. It is sometimes called the Vermont Piedmont. The region has broad, fertile lowlands where dairy cattle graze and apples and strawberries thrive. The western section has granite hills and quarries and forests that produce timber for lumber and paper products.

Vermont contains some of the largest granite quarries in the world. The Vermont Valley is also renowned for its fine white marble; near the New York border, excellent slate can be found.

Waitsfield, in north-central Vermont, is in the Green Mountain region. Beef cattle and maple syrup are among the agricultural products of this area.

The tree-covered Green Mountains, which give Vermont its nickname of Green Mountain State, range from the northern to the southern border in central Vermont. Oats, beef cattle, and maple syrup are produced here, and tourism is a major industry. Mount Mansfield, the highest point in the state at 4,393 feet, is in the Green Mountains.

Farms dot the tree-covered landscape of central Vermont, where the land supports beef, dairy, and fruit farms.

The Vermont Valley is a narrow strip of land located in the southwestern part of the state and extending about halfway up Vermont. This is dairy, fruit, maple-syrup, and forest-products country.

The Taconic Mountains rise more than 3,000 feet in southwestern Vermont and extend into Massachusetts. They have many swift-running streams and overlook tranquil lakes of unspoiled beauty. Some poultry is raised here, and potatoes are farmed.

The Champlain Valley, also called the Vermont Lowland, consists of a narrow strip in the northwestern part of the state that includes some of Vermont's best farmland. Dairy cattle are raised here, and farmers grow oats, potatoes, corn, hay, and fruit.

Vermont's winters are long: snow arrives before Christmas and lasts at least until early April. Some 64 inches of snow fall each year in southern Vermont, and accumulations may reach more than 82 inches in the mountainous northern regions.

Approximately 75 percent of Vermont's trees are hardwood, including maple, birch, basswood, and poplar. Farmers tapping the maple trees for syrup are a common sight during the late winter months.

The most important rivers of Vermont are the Connecticut, the Batten Kill, the Missisquoi, the Lamoille, the Winooski, and Otter Creek—the state's longest river. There are some 430 lakes and ponds in Vermont, most of them in the northeast. Lake Champlain, covering 490 square miles, is the largest in New England, and forms part of the border between Vermont and New York.

Vermont's climate is humid, with an annual precipitation of 35 to 45 inches. Much of this is in the form of snow, which may reach 120 inches in the Green Mountains. Winters are long and cold, with temperatures sometimes falling below 0 degrees Fahrenheit. Summers are cool and sunny. Rutland, in southern Vermont, has an average January temperature of about 20 degrees Fahrenheit; the July average is 70 degrees F. In Burlington, to the north, the January average is about 18 degrees F. and the July average 68 degrees F.

The History

Present-day Vermont was originally populated by Indians of the Abnaki, Mahican, and Pennacook tribes of the Algonquian language family. These tribes were hunters and farmers, whom invading Iroquois, from what is now New York State, drove out before the explorers came. They returned in the early 1600s, when the French helped them defeat the Iroquois.

In 1609 Frenchman Samuel de Champlain explored the large lake later named for him and claimed the Vermont region for France. In 1666 the French built a fort on Isle La Motte in Lake Champlain, south of their Canadian holdings, and in 1690 British soldiers from Albany, New York, established a fort at Chimney Point, near present-day Middlebury. The stage was set for decades of struggle between French and British claimants to the region. During the French and Indian Wars, which ended in 1763 in a British victory, the Lake Champlain region was a major battleground between the British and the French and their Indian allies.

Vermont was the last New England state to be settled, beginning in 1742, when Fort Drummer was built at what is now Brattleboro by Massachusetts settlers protecting their colony's western frontier.

Vermont land was also disputed among neighboring colonies between 1749 and 1770. The royal governor of New Hampshire made over 100 grants of Vermont land that was also claimed by New York, and settlers from both states moved in. The British government recognized the New York claim in 1764, ordering settlers who held New Hampshire Grants to give up their land or buy it from New York. This unpopular decision angered many settlers, and in 1770 a dissident military force called the Green Mountain Boys attacked New York settlers and drove them from Vermont.

When the Revolutionary War began in 1775, Vermonters united to back the rebellious colonists. Ethan Allen, Benedict Arnold, and more than 80 of the Green Mountain Boys made Vermont famous when they took Fort Ticonderoga from the British in 1775. Colonial troops occupied the fort until 1777, when they were driven out by the British. At the Battle of Bennington, fought in New York, just west of Vermont, on August 16, 1777, the British suffered a defeat that helped alter the course of the war.

Ethan Allen led Vermont's Green Mountain Boys in their fight to defend the region's land from settlement by New Yorkers. After the American Revolution began, Allen and his men joined forces with General Benedict Arnold to capture Fort Ticonderoga from the British on May 10, 1775.

British general John Burgoyne maneuvered his troops through the Ticonderoga and Saratoga regions during the summer of 1777. Although British forces scored a small victory when they surprised Vermont and New Hampshire troops at Hubbardton on July 7, Burgoyne was routed by General Horatio Gates's men. He surrendered at Saratoga, New York, on October 17, 1777.

Early in 1777, weary of arguments with New Hampshire and New York, Vermont settlers declared their region an independent republic, which they called New Connecticut. Six months later they adopted the name Vermont (from the French *Vert Mont*, or Green Mountain). They also drafted a state constitution which was unique in prohibiting human slavery and granting all males the right to vote, regardless of their property or income.

But Vermont's problems were not over. New Hampshire and New York still claimed parts of the republic. In 1783, when the Revolutionary War ended, George Washington considered sending troops to overthrow the Vermont government, but decided against it. Vermont remained an independent republic for 14 years, running its own postal service, coining its own money, naturalizing citizens of other states and countries, and negotiating with other states and nations. In 1790 New Hampshire finally gave up its claim to Vermont, and Vermont paid New York $30,000 for disputed territory. This cleared the way for Vermont to enter the Union in 1791 as the 14th state.

Many Vermont men fought in the War of 1812 with Great Britain, although the conflict was unpopular because Vermont had a great deal of trade with British Canada. After the war, the newly opened Champlain Canal, which connected the lake and New York's Hudson River, gave Vermont farmers a way to ship their goods south and rendered trade with Canada less important. Farmers prospered, and sheep raising became a big industry. When wool prices dropped in the mid-1800s, Vermont shifted to dairy farming.

Some 34,000 Vermont men served with Union forces during the Civil War, which began in 1861. And the war's northernmost action was fought in the state, when a group of 22 Confederate soldiers robbed banks in St. Albans and escaped to Canada with more than $20,000.

Although agriculture declined in Vermont after the Civil War ended in 1865, industry began to prosper, especially wood processing and cheese-making. Burlington became an important lumber port, and Barre was the center of a booming granite industry that supplied cut stone for buildings and monuments. Valuable marble deposits around Proctor and Rutland were quarried. By the early 1900s, Vermont was becoming more of a manufacturing than a farming state. Vermont lumber and machinery were important to the armed forces during World War I, which the United States entered in 1917.

Joseph Smith, a native of Sharon, Vermont, founded the Church of Jesus Christ of Latter-day Saints—the Mormon Church—in 1830. This faith was born at a time when several other religious groups, including the Millerites and the Perfectionists, originated in northern New England. During the 1820s and 1830s, these communities, with their radically new interpretations of the Bible, won many converts despite strong opposition from those who did not share their beliefs.

Montpelier, the state capital, is Vermont's third largest city. In recent years it has prospered from a year-round surge in tourism.

During the Great Depression of the 1930s, many Vermont factories and mills closed, some of them permanently. Small farms declined, and the trend toward larger farms would continue after economic recovery. When the United States entered World War II in 1941, Vermont factories increased their output of lumber, machinery, and other products, although the textile industry was adversely affected by Southern competition, as in other New England states.

Today Vermont is still growing economically. Major corporations have built factories in the state, and the tourist industry prospers in both summer and winter. The large resort hotels and vacation camps of the early 20th century have been joined by more than 56 ski areas that attract many visitors, especially to the Green Mountains.

The first free public school in Vermont opened in Guilford in 1761, and the Vermont constitution of 1777 required that each town have a public school. The first secondary school was established in Bennington in 1780. Vermont's first institution of higher education was the University of Vermont, founded in 1791. Middlebury College (1800) and Norwich University (1819) soon followed. Today the state has nine colleges and universities.

The People

Almost 34 percent of the people in Vermont live in towns and cities, including Burlington, Rutland, Barre, and Montpelier. Most of them were born in the United States, and more than half of those born elsewhere came from Canada. The largest religious group in the state consists of Roman Catholics. Other large denominations are the United Church of Christ, Methodists, Baptists, and Episcopalians.

Thaddeus Stevens, born in the frontier village of Danville, was a prominent politician during the Civil War and Reconstruction eras. Stevens opposed slavery and fought bitterly against any compromise with the South during the crisis of 1860–61, which culminated in the Civil War.

Chester A. Arthur, the 21st president of the United States, was born in Fairfield, Vermont.

At left:
Calvin Coolidge, a native of Plymouth Notch, was America's 30th president. He succeeded President Warren G. Harding, who died in office in 1923. During his six years in the White House, Coolidge improved relations with Mexico and supported American business at home and abroad.

Above:
Robert Frost, best known for his poems about rural New England, won the Pulitzer Prize for poetry in 1924, 1931, 1937, and 1943. In January 1961 he read one of his poems at the inauguration of President Kennedy.

Two Vermonters have become president of the United States: Chester Alan Arthur of Fairfield, the 21st president, and Calvin Coolidge of Plymouth, the 30th. Admiral George Dewey, the hero of the Battle of Manila Bay during the Spanish-American War, was a native of Montpelier. Educational philosopher John Dewey, who taught that all ideas must be tested by experience, was born in Burlington. Senator Stephen A. Douglas, a renowned orator who ran for president against Abraham Lincoln, came from Brandon.

The paddlewheeler S.S. *Ticonderoga* is part of the Shelburne Museum.

OF SPECIAL INTEREST

IN BENNINGTON: *Bennington Battle Monument*
A 306-foot-high granite tower honors the colonists who won the Battle of Bennington in 1777. This is the world's second tallest battle monument.

IN PROCTOR: *Vermont Marble Exhibit*
This exhibit at one of the world's largest marble quarrying centers features a unique collection of various kinds of marble.

IN WINDSOR: *Old Constitution House*
Vermont's first constitution was written in this two-story frame house, built as a tavern in 1772.

IN SHELBURNE: *Shelburne Museum*
This reconstruction of an early American village features a large collection of furnishings, tools, toys, and other items used by Vermont's early settlers.

IN PLYMOUTH: *Coolidge Homestead*
The museum at the birthplace of America's 30th president houses mementoes of his life and political career.

For more information write:
VERMONT TRAVEL DIVISION
134 STATE STREET
MONTPELIER, VERMONT 05602

FURTHER READING

Carpenter, Allan. *Vermont*, rev. ed. Childrens Press, 1979.

Cheney, Cora: *Vermont: The State with the Storybook Past*. Stephen Greene Press, 1976.

Fradin, Dennis B. *Vermont in Words and Pictures*. Childrens Press, 1980

Hill, Ralph N. *Contrary Country: A Chronicle of Vermont*. Stephen Greene Press, 1974.

Johnson, Charles W. *The Nature of Vermont: Introduction and Guide to a New England Environment*. University Press of New England, 1980.

Morrissey, Charles T. *Vermont: A Bicentennial History*. W.W. Norton, 1980.

INDEX

Numbers in italics refer to illustrations

63

Photo Credits/Acknowledgments

Photos on pages 5, 6–7, 9, 10, 12, 13, courtesy of Joseph Devenney/Maine Office of Tourism; pages 14, 16, Library of Congress; pages 18, 22, 36, 40, Richard Glassman; pages 19, 20, 21, National Portrait Gallery; pages 23, 30 (right), David Brownell; pages 24–25, 28, M. T. Pinkerton; pages 29, 34, 39 (left), New Hampshire Office of Vacation Travel; page 30 (left), William Johnson; pages 33, 37, 38 (right), National Portrait Gallery; page 35, Stokes Collection, New York Public Library; page 39 (right), J. Northrup Bennet; pages 41, 42–43, 45, 46, 47, 48, 49, 50, 51, 52, 58, 62, Vermont Travel Division; pages 54, 55, 61 (right), Library of Congress; pages 57, 59, 60, 61 (left), National Portrait Gallery.

Cover photograph courtesy of R. Glassman.

The Publisher would like to thank Cheryl Burdzel of the Maine Office of Tourism, Ann Kennard of the New Hampshire Office of Vacation Travel, and Amanda Sessel Legare and William Braun of the Vermont Office of Vacation Travel for their gracious assistance in the preparation of this book.